Level C · Book 1

QuickReads®

A Research-Based Fluency Program

Elfrieda H. Hiebert, Ph.D.

MODERN CURRICULUM PRESS

Pearson Learning Group

Program Reviewers and Consultants

Dr. Barbara A. Baird
Director of Federal Programs/Richardson ISD
Richardson, TX

Dr. Kate Kinsella
Dept. of Secondary Education and Step to College Program
San Francisco State University
San Francisco, CA

Pat Sears
Early Child Coordinator/Virginia Beach Public Schools
Virginia Beach, VA

Dr. Judith B. Smith
Supervisor of ESOL and World and Classical Languages/Baltimore City Public Schools
Baltimore, MD

The following people have contributed to the development of this product:

Art and Design: Adriano Farinella, Luis Ferreira, Dorothea Fox, Salita Mehta,
  Janice Noto-Helmers, Dan Thomas

Editorial: Lynn W. Kloss

Manufacturing: Michele Uhl

Marketing: Connie Buck

Production: Laura Benford-Sullivan, Jeffrey Engel

Publishing Operations: Jennifer Van Der Heide

Acknowledgments appear on page 9, which constitutes an extension of this copyright page.

QuickReads® is a registered trademark of Pearson Education, Inc.

ISBN 0-7652-2741-X

Printed in the United States of America

15 16 17 - 10 09 08 07

Modern Curriculum Press
Pearson Learning Group

1-800-321-3106
www.pearsonlearning.com

Contents

SCIENCE **Dinosaurs**

Dinosaur Names 10

Finding Out About Dinosaurs 12

Meat-Eating Dinosaurs 14

Plant-Eating Dinosaurs 16

A Very Small Dinosaur. 18

Dinosaurs Review 20

 Connect Your Ideas 23

Contents

SCIENCE **Animal Giants**

Ocean Giants: Blue Whales 24

Land Giants: Elephants 26

Bird Giants: Ostriches .28

Tall Giants: Giraffes 30

Long Giants: Saltwater Crocodiles 32

Animal Giants Review .34

 Connect Your Ideas 37

SCIENCE **Plants**

The Parts of Plants 38

How Plants Breathe 40

Why Are Flowers Beautiful? 42

Dangerous Plants 44

Growing Your Own Plants 46

Plants Review 48

 Connect Your Ideas 51

Contents

SOCIAL STUDIES

American Heroes

George Washington 52

Martin Luther King, Jr. 54

Clara Barton 56

César Chávez 58

Wilma Rudolph 60

American Heroes Review 62

 Connect Your Ideas .65

SOCIAL
STUDIES

Celebrations

What Is a Celebration? 66

Thanksgiving 68

A Birthday Party for the United States 70

Thinking About the Past 72

Celebrating New Year's Day 74

Celebrations Review .76

Connect Your Ideas 79

Contents

SOCIAL STUDIES

Our National Government

Who's in Charge of Our Country? 80

Leading the Way 82

Making the Laws 84

Helping People Understand the Laws 86

Our Nation's Capital 88

Our National Government Review 90

 Connect Your Ideas 93

Reading Log 94

Self-Check Graph 96

Acknowledgments

All photographs © Pearson Learning unless otherwise noted.

Cover: William S. Helsel/Tony Stone Images.

3: Shiraishi Mineo. 4: D. & OSF Bartlett/Animals Animals/Earth Scenes. 5: Darrell Gulin/DRK Photo. 6: AP/Wide World Photos. 7: U.S. Department of Defense. 8: © Joseph Sohm/Visions of America/Corbis. 10: © Bettmann/Corbis. 12: © AFP/Corbis. 14: Shiraishi Mineo. 16: Shiraishi Mineo. 18: Shiraishi Mineo. 24: Flip Nicklin/Minden Pictures. 26: Pearson Learning. 28: D. & OSF Bartlett/Animals Animals/Earth Scenes. 30: Gregory G. Dimijian/Photo Researchers, Inc. 32: SuperStock, Inc. 38: Darrell Gulin/DRK Photo. 40: SuperStock, Inc. 42: © Darwin Dale/Photo Researchers, Inc. 44: Mickey Gibson/Animals Animals/Earth Scenes. 46: © Helen Norman/Corbis. 52: AP/Wide World Photo. 54: CNP/Archive Photos. 56: Pearson Learning. 58: © Bettmann/Corbis. 60: © Bettmann/Corbis. 66: © Myrleen Ferguson Cate/PhotoEdit. 68: The Granger Collection. 70: Ariel Skelley/Corbis Stock Market. 72: U.S. Department of Defense. 74: San Francisco Convention and Visitors Bureau. 80: Library of Congress. 82: Win McNamee/AP/Wide World Photos. 84: Kenneth Lambert/AP/Wide World Photos. 86: Washington Stock Photo, Inc. 88: © Joseph Sohm/Visions of America/Corbis

Millions of years ago, many different
kinds of dinosaurs lived on Earth.

Daniel

Dinosaur Names

Dinosaurs were animals that lived on Earth millions and millions of years ago. No dinosaurs are living today on Earth.

When the first bones of a dinosaur were found, people thought that they had found a very big lizard. The word *saur* means "lizard." The word *dino* means "something to fear." Put the words *dino* and *saur* together. You get the word "dinosaur," or "big lizard to fear."

Since those first bones were found, the bones of many kinds of dinosaurs have been found. Each kind of dinosaur has a different name, but many of them have *saur* in their names.

Paleontologists have found many dinosaur bones.

Finding Out About Dinosaurs

How do we know that dinosaurs lived long, long ago? There are people who find out about dinosaurs. They are called [25]paleontologists. Paleontologists learn about dinosaurs from fossils. Fossils are the things left over from long ago, such as dinosaur bones and eggs. Fossils are found[50] under the ground and in rocks. Paleontologists dig in the ground and look at rocks to find fossils.

By looking at fossils, paleontologists can learn[75]if a dinosaur was small or large. Fossils also help paleontologists learn where a dinosaur lived on land, how fast it moved, and what it ate.[101]

Dinosaurs

Tyrannosaurus rex was a big meat-eating dinosaur.

Meat-Eating Dinosaurs

The teeth that are found in fossils help us know what dinosaurs ate. When dinosaur teeth are long and sharp, we know[25] that these dinosaurs ate meat.

Meat-eating dinosaurs came in many sizes. The dinosaurs' long, strong legs helped them run after other animals. Meat-eating[50] dinosaurs had short arms. Their arms ended in sharp claws. These sharp claws were used to tear at other animals.

One of the biggest of[75] the meat-eating dinosaurs was Tyrannosaurus rex. The word *rex* means "king." We call Tyrannosaurus rex the "king of the dinosaurs" because of its large size.[101]

Dinosaurs

Brachiosaurus was a very tall plant-eating dinosaur.

Plant-Eating Dinosaurs

When the teeth in fossils are flat, we know that these dinosaurs ate plants. Some of the biggest dinosaurs were plant eaters.[25] They were even bigger than Tyrannosaurus rex. Tall plant-eating dinosaurs ate leaves from the tops of trees. Short plant-eating dinosaurs ate plants near[50] the ground.

One big plant-eater was the Brachiosaurus. Brachiosaurus was one of the biggest dinosaurs. It was taller than a three-story building. It[75] had a long, thin neck so that it could reach even the tallest trees. Its long neck helped Brachiosaurus reach food that other plant-eating dinosaurs could not.[104]

Dinosaurs

The Saltopus was a small meat-eating dinosaur.

A Very Small Dinosaur

When you think about dinosaurs, you might think about animals that were huge. Yet some dinosaurs were small. One was as [25] small as a cat that you might have for a pet. This dinosaur was called the Saltopus.

The Saltopus was an early dinosaur. Because it [50] lived so long ago, paleontologists do not know much about the Saltopus. They do know that the Saltopus was a meat eater. It may have [75] eaten insects and dead animals. They also know that the Saltopus had many small, sharp teeth and could run very fast. The Saltopus doesn't sound like a good pet! [104]

Dinosaurs

Write words that will help you remember what you learned.

Dinosaur Names

saur means
lisrd
dino means
to fear

Finding Out About Dinosaurs

Paleontologists
Fossils
bons and ag
e

Meat-Eating Dinosaurs

Plant-Eating Dinosaurs

A Very Small Dinosaur

Dinosaur Names

1. "Dinosaur Names" is MAINLY about _B_

   Ⓐ when dinosaurs lived.

   Ⓑ the meaning of dinosaur names.

   Ⓒ where dinosaur bones were found.

   Ⓓ the parts of dinosaurs.

2. Retell what you learned in "Dinosaur Names."

   I learned uabout
   saur and bino

   _____

Finding Out About Dinosaurs

1. Choose another name for "Finding Out About Dinosaurs."

   Ⓐ "Paleontologists Like Dinosaurs"

   Ⓑ "Dinosaurs Are Large"

   Ⓒ "Fossils Are Old"

   Ⓓ "Fossils Tell About the Past"

2. How do paleontologists find out about dinosaurs?

   Thay look For D Fossils.
   Fing Thay Finde Fosils thay nowat
   thay eat

   Dinosaurs tho Fast

Dinosaurs

Meat-Eating Dinosaurs

1. "Meat-Eating Dinosaurs" is MAINLY about ____

Ⓐ Tyrannosaurus rex.

Ⓑ the way paleontologists learn about fossils.

Ⓒ what meat-eating dinosaurs were like.

Ⓓ how meat-eating dinosaurs walked.

2. How did meat-eating dinosaurs look and act?

Thay had shrp teeth and clos Thay chast othr Dinosaurs!!

Plant-Eating Dinosaurs

1. The thing that is the same about all plant-eating dinosaurs is ____

Ⓐ they all were called Brachiosaurus.

Ⓑ they all were big.

Ⓒ they all ate trees.

Ⓓ they all had flat teeth.

2. How did plant-eating dinosaurs look and act?

thay all had flaT teeth and ate levs.

22

A Very Small Dinosaur

1. What is the most important idea in "A Very Small Dinosaur"?

Ⓐ The Saltopus was a small meat-eating dinosaur.

Ⓑ The Saltopus was just like a pet cat from today.

Ⓒ The Saltopus was friendly to other dinosaurs.

Ⓓ The Saltopus ate plants and animals.

2. How did the Saltopus look and act?

_____

_____

_____

Connect Your Ideas

1. How are the dinosaurs alike that are described in these readings?

_____

_____

_____

2. How are they different?

_____

_____

_____

Blue whales are animal giants of the ocean.

Ocean Giants: Blue Whales

The giant of all animals on Earth is the blue whale. At 100 feet long, it is longer than two school[25] buses. To be as heavy as a blue whale, the two school buses would need to have 2,000 people in them.

The blue whale gets[50] its food by keeping its mouth open as it swims. There are big plates in its mouth. When the blue whale's mouth is full of[75] water and tiny sea animals, it shuts its mouth. Then it pushes the water out through the plates. The animals stay inside the whale's mouth. It's lunch time![103]

Elephants are animal giants that live on land.

Land Giants: Elephants

The giant of the animals that live on land is the elephant. Think of three cars, one on top of another. One [25] elephant would be the same size—about 12 feet high and weighing more than five tons. Even the ears of an elephant are big. An [50] elephant's ears can be as wide as you are tall—four feet!

To get down low or reach up high, the elephant gets help from [75] its trunk. An elephant can swing its trunk to the ground to get water. It can also swing its trunk high into the trees to get food. [102]

Animal Giants

Ostriches are giant birds.

Bird Giants: Ostriches

Big Bird on TV is not real, but there is a bird that is real and is even bigger than Big Bird.[25] Ostriches are the giants of birds. They can grow to eight feet tall. The top of an ostrich's head would hit the top of most[50] rooms in a house. Its neck can be as long as four feet.

Most birds can fly, but ostriches are too heavy to fly. Their[75] wings cannot hold them up. However, ostriches can run very fast. They are the fastest animals on two feet. They can run faster than even the fastest people can.[104]

Animal Giants

Giraffes are long-necked giants.

Tall Giants: Giraffes

Giraffes are the tallest animals on Earth. They can grow to be 18 feet tall. Giraffes are as tall or taller than [25] many houses. Their long necks and legs let them eat the leaves of trees that other animals cannot reach.

The long legs of giraffes help [50] them run very fast. Giraffes can run up to 30 miles per hour. Yet their long legs make it hard for giraffes to drink. Because [75] giraffes are so tall, they have to bend far over to reach the ground. So when they need water, they have to bend very far to get a drink. [104]

Saltwater crocodiles are reptiles with long bodies.

Long Giants:
Saltwater Crocodiles

Some of the longest animals on Earth are reptiles such as snakes and crocodiles. Snakes are reptiles that have no legs.[25] Other reptiles, like crocodiles, have very short legs.

These reptiles make up for their short legs with long bodies. One of the longest reptiles is[50] the saltwater crocodile. Saltwater crocodiles can grow up to 20 feet long. That is as long as five or six children in a row. Saltwater[75] crocodiles can attack large animals. They use their teeth when they attack. Yet mother crocodiles are very careful with their babies. They even carry their babies in their mouths.[104]

Animal Giants

Write words that will help you remember what you learned.

Ocean Giants: Blue Whales

_____

_____

_____

_____

Land Giants: Elephants

_____

_____

_____

_____

Bird Giants: Ostriches

_____

_____

_____

_____

Tall Giants: Giraffes

_____

_____

_____

_____

**Long Giants:
Saltwater Crocodiles**

_____

_____

_____

_____

Ocean Giants: Blue Whales

1. Another good name for "Ocean Giants: Blue Whales" is _____

Ⓐ "Blue Whales Are Good Pets."

Ⓑ "Blue Whales Are Like School Buses."

Ⓒ "Blue Whales Are Huge Sea Animals."

Ⓓ "Blue Whales Eat Fish."

2. Describe blue whales.

_____

_____

_____

Land Giants: Elephants

1. You could read "Land Giants: Elephants" to learn about _____

Ⓐ how big elephants are.

Ⓑ where elephants live.

Ⓒ how elephants walk.

Ⓓ how elephants swing their trunks.

2. What two things can elephants do with their trunks?

_____

_____

_____

Bird Giants: Ostriches

1. What is one special thing about ostriches?

Ⓐ They can fly very fast.

Ⓑ They are very tall.

Ⓒ They can see very well.

Ⓓ They are very good hunters.

2. How do ostriches move around?

_____

_____

_____

Tall Giants: Giraffes

1. "Tall Giants: Giraffes" is MAINLY about _____

Ⓐ the size of giraffes.

Ⓑ the color of giraffes.

Ⓒ how giraffes run.

Ⓓ how giraffes drink.

2. How do their long necks and legs help giraffes?

_____

_____

_____

Long Giants: Saltwater Crocodiles

1. Which part of saltwater crocodiles is very long?

Ⓐ their bodies

Ⓑ their legs

Ⓒ their noses

Ⓓ their teeth

2. Retell what you learned about saltwater crocodiles.

_____

_____

_____

Connect Your Ideas

1. Do you think that *Animal Giants* is a good title for these readings? Why or why not?

_____

_____

_____

2. Describe another animal giant that you know about.

_____

_____

_____

Plants

There are many different kinds of plants on Earth.

The Parts of Plants

A tree in a forest and a water lily floating on a pond don't look alike. But both a tree and[25] a water lily share things that make them plants.

Plants are living things. Most plants have roots, a stem, and leaves. Roots get the plant[50] water and minerals from the soil. The stem brings water and minerals from the roots to the rest of the plant. Leaves take in parts[75] of the air that plants need to live. The roots, stems, and leaves of different plants may not look alike, but most plants have the same parts.[102]

Plants

Both plants and animals need air to live.

How Plants Breathe

Did you know that plants, animals, and people all need air to stay alive? Plants use air differently than people and animals.[25] Yet like people and animals, plants need air to stay alive.

When people and animals breathe in, they take oxygen from the air into their[50] lungs. When they breathe out, they let carbon dioxide out of their lungs. When plants breathe, they take in carbon dioxide from the air, and[75] they let oxygen out. Plants don't have lungs like people. They use their leaves to breathe. Plants, animals, and people trade oxygen and carbon dioxide to help each other breathe.[105]

Bees carry pollen from flower to flower.

Why Are Flowers Beautiful?

Flowers bloom in bright colors and different shapes. The bright colors and shapes of flowers are important to the life of [25] a plant. The colors, shapes, and smells of flowers make them interesting to insects.

Flowers need insects to pollinate them so they can grow seeds. [50] Insects pick up a sticky powder when they stop near the center of a flower. This powder is called pollen. Each time insects land on [75] a flower, they leave the powder, or pollen, behind. Once it is pollinated, a plant grows seeds. Later, these seeds fall to the ground. New flowers grow from these seeds. [105]

This bird has learned how to
stay safe from the plant's thorns.

Dangerous Plants

We usually don't think of plants as dangerous. Yet parts of some plants can be poisonous. Other plants have thorns that can hurt[25] people and animals. These poisonous or thorny parts keep the seeds of plants from being eaten or harmed.

We eat the part of the potato[50] plant that grows underground. This underground part is safe to eat. Yet the leaves and flowers of the potato plant above the ground are poisonous.[75] Roses are beautiful flowers, but their bushes have sharp thorns. An animal that tries to eat a rose may get a mouthful of thorns for dinner![101]

Sunflowers can be easy to grow.

Growing Your Own Plants

Plants come in many shapes and sizes. Some have beautiful flowers. Some have lots of green leaves. Some grow fruit.

One [25] plant that is easy to grow is the sunflower. Plant your sunflower seeds where they will get lots of sunlight. Seeds should be planted a [50] foot from each other and a half-inch deep. Water the soil so that it does not dry out. Put some net over the soil [75] until the plants grow above ground. A net will keep birds from eating your sunflower seeds. In late summer, your sunflowers will be ready to pick. [101]

Plants

Write words that will help you remember what you learned.

The Parts of Plants

_____

_____

_____

_____

How Plants Breathe

_____

_____

_____

_____

Why Are Flowers Beautiful?

_____

_____

_____

_____

Dangerous Plants

_____

_____

_____

_____

Growing Your Own Plants

_____

_____

_____

_____

The Parts of Plants

1. Another good name for "The Parts of Plants" is _____

    Ⓐ "Stems and Leaves."

    Ⓑ "What Do Plants Eat?"

    Ⓒ "How Plants Are Alike."

    Ⓓ "Cactus Plants."

2. How are most plants alike?

_____

_____

_____

How Plants Breathe

1. What do plants, animals, and people need to live?

    Ⓐ carbon dioxide

    Ⓑ air

    Ⓒ oxygen

    Ⓓ lungs

2. How do plants breathe?

_____

_____

_____

Why Are Flowers Beautiful?

1. What makes a plant interesting to insects?

Ⓐ the colors, shapes, and smells of flowers

Ⓑ the pollen of the flower

Ⓒ the seeds of the plant

Ⓓ the other insects on the plant

2. How do insects pollinate flowers?

_____

_____

_____

Dangerous Plants

1. Being dangerous helps a plant by _____

Ⓐ making it beautiful.

Ⓑ helping it find food.

Ⓒ making it hard to reach.

Ⓓ keeping people and animals away.

2. Name two ways that a plant can be dangerous.

_____

_____

_____

Growing Your Own Plants

1. What is the first thing to do when you plant sunflowers?

   Ⓐ Choose a place where they will get rain.

   Ⓑ Choose a place where they will get sunlight.

   Ⓒ Choose a place where birds won't find them.

   Ⓓ Choose a place where you can see their flowers.

2. Describe how to grow sunflowers.

   _____

   _____

   _____

Connect Your Ideas

1. What would you tell someone who wanted to learn about plants?

   _____

   _____

   _____

2. Name two ways that plants and animals are alike.

   _____

   _____

   _____

George Washington was the first American president.

George Washington

A hero is someone who does brave and important things. George Washington was one of the first American heroes. He was the general[25] of the American army that won the war against the British. Sometimes it seemed that the American army would win. Sometimes it seemed the army[50] would lose. Yet General George Washington did not give up until America won the war.

In 1789, George Washington became the first American president. As[75] the first president, he had to do many new things. He had to find ways to run the new country. George Washington is an American hero.[101]

Martin Luther King, Jr., worked for the rights of all Americans.

Martin Luther King, Jr.

Not long ago, some Americans did not have the same rights as other Americans. In some places, African American children could not[25] go to school with other children. There were rules that made it hard for African American people to vote. Martin Luther King, Jr., said that[50] all Americans should have the same rights. He made many speeches. One speech was about his dream for America.

Martin Luther King, Jr., was put[75] in jail. Yet he still worked for the rights of all Americans. He helped many people get all of their rights. Martin Luther King, Jr., is an American hero.[104]

Clara Barton started the American Red Cross.

Clara Barton

Around the world, the Red Cross stands for help in bad times like storms or wars. There has not always been a Red[25]Cross in the United States. We can thank Clara Barton for starting the American Red Cross.

When the Civil War started, Clara Barton left her[50]home to be a nurse in the war. When the Civil War ended, she became a nurse in a war in Europe. While in Europe,[75] she saw how the Red Cross helped people. When she came home to the United States, Clara Barton started the American Red Cross. She is an American hero.[103]

César Chávez helped farm workers have better lives.

César Chávez

When César Chávez and his family lost their farm, they picked fruit for other farmers. César Chávez could not be in one school[25] for very long because his family needed to move to a new place to pick the fruit there. Picking fruit is hard work. The days[50] are hot and long.

As César Chávez grew older, he saw that farm workers needed health care and better pay. He worked so that people[75] could have better lives. Today, many farm workers have health care and better pay because of César Chávez's hard work. César Chávez is an American hero.[101]

Wilma Rudolph won three Olympic gold medals.

Wilma Rudolph

When Wilma Rudolph was young, she got very sick. She got better, but one leg was so weak that she could not walk.[25] Every day, her family rubbed her weak leg. One day, she could walk with a brace on her leg. Then, she needed only a special[50] shoe. One day, she could walk without the special shoe.

Wilma Rudolph loved to run. When she grew up, Wilma Rudolph ran so fast that[75] she won medals at many races. At the 1960 Olympics, she was the first American woman to win three gold medals at one Olympics. Wilma Rudolph is an American hero.[105]

American Heroes

Write words that will help you remember what you learned.

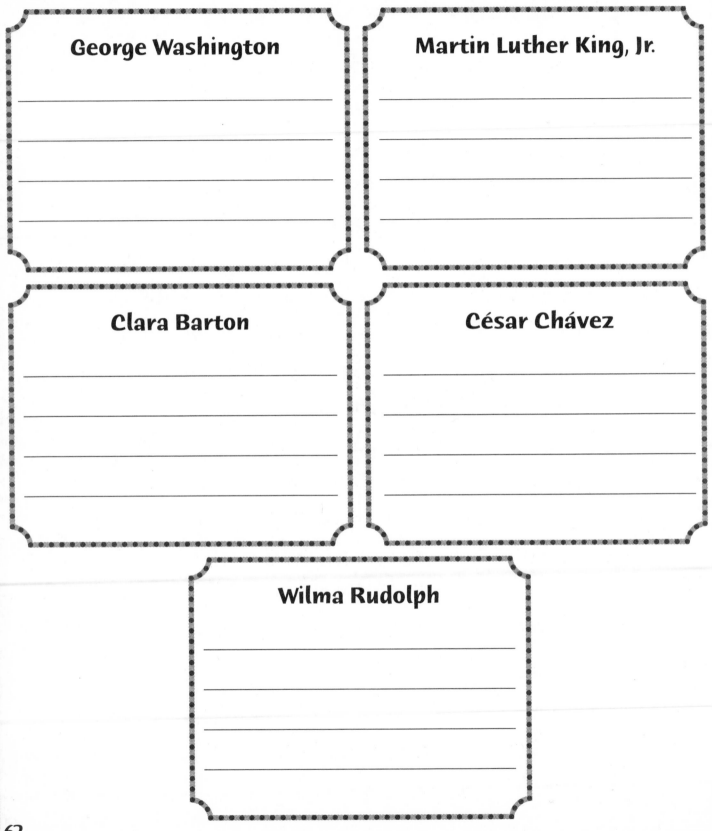

George Washington

Martin Luther King, Jr.

Clara Barton

César Chávez

Wilma Rudolph

George Washington

1. "George Washington" is MAINLY about _____

Ⓐ how George Washington became president.

Ⓑ how George Washington won the war.

Ⓒ the important things that George Washington did.

Ⓓ what George Washington did when he was president.

2. Why is George Washington an American hero?

_____

_____

_____

Martin Luther King, Jr.

1. Martin Luther King, Jr., is a hero because _____

Ⓐ he was able to vote.

Ⓑ he was a good speaker.

Ⓒ he had good ideas.

Ⓓ he worked for all people's rights.

2. Retell what you learned about Martin Luther King, Jr.

_____

_____

_____

American Heroes

Clara Barton

1. Another good name for "Clara Barton" is _____

Ⓐ "Clara Barton Was a Nurse."

Ⓑ "The Red Cross in Europe."

Ⓒ "The Red Cross Today."

Ⓓ "Clara Barton Helped People."

2. Describe two ways Clara Barton helped people.

_____

_____

_____

César Chávez

1. What is the most important idea in "César Chávez"?

Ⓐ César Chávez was a farm worker.

Ⓑ César Chávez picked fruit.

Ⓒ César Chávez's family lost its farm.

Ⓓ César Chávez made people's lives better.

2. How did César Chávez help people?

_____

_____

_____

Wilma Rudolph

1. "Wilma Rudolph" is MAINLY about how Wilma Rudolph _____

   Ⓐ loved to run.

   Ⓑ learned to walk.

   Ⓒ won gold medals.

   Ⓓ got well.

2. Why is Wilma Rudolph an American hero?

_____

_____

_____

Connect Your Ideas

1. How are these American heroes alike?

_____

_____

_____

2. Tell what you think it means to be a hero.

_____

_____

_____

Celebrations

Birthday parties are one kind of celebration.

What Is a Celebration?

It's your birthday. Your friends are coming to your house for a party. There will be lots of food to eat.[25] You and your friends will play games. They may even give you gifts. It's your special day!

There are also special times when many people[50] have a party. These special times are called celebrations. On some celebrations, people do not go to work. There is no school. Most celebrations are[75] happy ones, like New Year's Day. However, there are also celebrations, such as Memorial Day, when we think of sad things that happened in the past.[101]

Celebrations

On Thanksgiving, we celebrate how
Native Americans helped the Pilgrims.

Thanksgiving

In America many years ago, people worked hard to grow enough food to last all winter. In most places, the winter weather was too [25] cold for growing food. In the fall, when all of the food was stored, people celebrated. Today most people do not grow their own food. [50] However, we still have a day of thanksgiving.

On Thanksgiving, Americans think about how the Native Americans helped the settlers called the Pilgrims. The Pilgrims [75] did not know how to grow food in their new land. The Native Americans showed the settlers how to grow enough food to feed themselves all year. [102]

Celebrations

Many towns have parades that celebrate Independence Day.

A Birthday Party for the United States

In the United States, we celebrate the day on which our country was first set up. This day[25] is called Independence Day. Independence Day is the birthday party for our country.

On Independence Day, we have different ways to celebrate our country's birthday.[50] Many people fly the red, white, and blue flag of our country on their houses. Many towns have parades. Bands play music in the parades.[75] At night on Independence Day, many towns set off fireworks. Fireworks light up the sky with color. Fireworks often are red, white, and blue, just like our country's flag.[104]

Celebrations

Some celebrations help us remember people
who have fought for our country.

Thinking About the Past

Most celebrations are happy times. However, on some days, we celebrate other things that happened in the past. One of these [25] days is Veterans Day, which happens in the fall of the year. On Veterans Day, we stop and think about those people who fought for [50] our country.

On Memorial Day, we think about people who died or were hurt in wars. Memorial Day is in the spring of the year. [75] Veterans Day and Memorial Day are times when we think about the people who have fought for our country. We celebrate what they have done for us. [102]

Celebrations

Chinese New Year is often celebrated with a parade.

Celebrating New Year's Day

In many countries, the first day of the new year is a time of celebration. People start the new year[25] with food, parades, and parties.

All countries do not start the new year on the same day. In China, the new year begins on a[50] different day than it does in the United States. It also begins on a different day each year. On their new year's day, people in[75] China have family celebrations. They give each other gifts.

People in many countries celebrate the start of a new year. They just don't begin their year on the same day.[105]

Celebrations

Write words that will help you remember what you learned.

What Is a Celebration?

_____
_____
_____
_____

Thanksgiving

_____
_____
_____
_____

A Birthday Party for the United States

_____
_____
_____
_____

Thinking About the Past

_____
_____
_____
_____

Celebrating New Year's Day

_____
_____
_____
_____

What Is a Celebration?

1. Another good name for "What Is a Celebration?" is _____

 Ⓐ "Celebrations Are Special Times."

 Ⓑ "Birthdays Are Celebrations."

 Ⓒ "Celebrations Are Times for Parties."

 Ⓓ "New Year's Day Is a Celebration."

2. Describe two celebrations.

_____

_____

_____

Thanksgiving

1. What is the most important idea in "Thanksgiving"?

 Ⓐ when Thanksgiving happens

 Ⓑ how to grow food for Thanksgiving

 Ⓒ why we celebrate Thanksgiving

 Ⓓ what people eat on Thanksgiving

2. Retell what you learned about Thanksgiving.

_____

_____

_____

A Birthday Party for the United States

1. "A Birthday Party for the United States" is MAINLY about _____

Ⓐ how people celebrate Independence Day.

Ⓑ the colors of the United States flag.

Ⓒ fireworks and parades.

Ⓓ when people celebrate Independence Day.

2. What is Independence Day?

_____

_____

_____

Thinking About the Past

1. "Thinking About the Past" tells MAINLY about _____

Ⓐ happy celebrations.

Ⓑ days we celebrate people who have been brave.

Ⓒ Memorial Day celebrations.

Ⓓ people who fought for our country.

2. Why do we celebrate Veterans Day and Memorial Day?

_____

_____

_____

Celebrating New Year's Day

1. Another good name for "Celebrating New Year's Day" is _____

   Ⓐ "New Year's Day Is the First Day of the Year."

   Ⓑ "Everyone Celebrates New Year's Day."

   Ⓒ "People Celebrate New Year's Day in Different Ways."

   Ⓓ "New Year's Day Is a Day for Parties."

2. What is New Year's Day?

   _____

   _____

   _____

 **Connect Your Ideas**

1. Compare two of the celebrations you have read about.

   _____

   _____

   _____

2. Describe a celebration that you know.

   _____

   _____

   _____

These people are planning the first government of the United States.

Who's in Charge of Our Country?

We think of the president as the head of our country. However, the president must work with other leaders[25] to run our nation. Our national government has three branches. One branch makes the laws. Another branch makes sure the country's laws are being followed.[50] The third branch helps us understand those laws.

On a baseball team, the pitcher and the catcher have different jobs. Like the pitcher and catcher[75] on a baseball team, the people who work in each branch of government have different jobs. Also, everyone in the government must work together to get the job done.[104]

The president leads one branch of the United States government. This picture shows President George W. Bush.

Leading the Way

The first branch of our national government is led by the president. The president has several jobs. The president gives ideas about [25] spending money and making new laws for our country. The president is in charge of the armed forces like the army. The president also makes [50] sure that the laws of our country are followed. Another job of the president is to work with the leaders of other countries.

The president [75] does not work alone. Many other people also work for this branch of government. These people have jobs like caring for our national parks or taking care of taxes. [104]

Congress makes the laws in the United States. Congress is the second branch of the United States government.

Making the Laws

Schools have rules like "Don't run in the halls." Rules help keep people safe. Our nation has rules that are called laws.[25] Our nation's laws are made by Congress, the second branch of government.

Congress has two parts: the Senate and the House of Representatives. Each state[50] elects two senators. Because the United States has 50 states, there are 100 senators. Each state elects different numbers of people to the House of[75] Representatives. This is because some states are bigger than others. States with many people like New York have more representatives in the House than states with few people like Maine.[105]

There are nine judges on the Supreme Court.

Helping People Understand the Laws

Have you ever played in a game in which teams did not agree on a rule? When that happens, an[25] umpire decides what the rules mean. The third branch of our government is the Supreme Court. The Supreme Court acts like an umpire when there[50] are different ideas about a law. Supreme Court judges are the only leaders of our nation who are not elected.

The nine judges of the[75] Supreme Court hear ideas about laws from people or states. Only five of the nine judges need to agree for the Supreme Court to decide what a law means.[104]

Congress meets in the United States
Capitol building in Washington, D.C.

Our Nation's Capital

Leaders in all three branches of our national government work together in our nation's capital, Washington, D.C. The president lives and works[25] in the White House. This building is a big, white house. There are also many offices throughout Washington, D.C., where people work on jobs for[50] the president, like taking care of taxes.

The U.S. Capitol building in Washington, D.C., has two very large parts. The Senators meet and work in[75] one part and the Representatives meet and work in the other part. Close to the U.S. Capitol building is the Supreme Court building. It has a courtroom and many offices.[105]

REVIEW   Our National Government

Write words that will help you remember what you learned.

Who's in Charge of Our Country?

_____

_____

_____

Leading the Way

_____

_____

_____

_____

Making the Laws

_____

_____

_____

Helping People Understand the Laws

_____

_____

_____

Our Nation's Capital

_____

_____

_____

_____

Who's in Charge of Our Country?

1. "Who's in Charge of Our Country?" is MAINLY about _____

Ⓐ baseball teams.

Ⓑ the president of the United States.

Ⓒ how the United States government is set up.

Ⓓ the branches of a tree.

2. Who is in charge of our country?

_____

_____

_____

Leading the Way

1. Another good name for "Leading the Way" is _____

Ⓐ "The President's Jobs."

Ⓑ "The President Works in the Army."

Ⓒ "The Leaders of Other Countries."

Ⓓ "The President Works Alone."

2. Describe two things that the president does.

_____

_____

_____

Making the Laws

1. What does Congress do?

   Ⓐ Congress makes the nation's laws.

   Ⓑ Congress runs the branches of government.

   Ⓒ Congress elects the Senate.

   Ⓓ Congress makes school laws.

2. What are the two parts of Congress?

_____

_____

_____

Helping People Understand the Laws

1. What does the Supreme Court do?

   Ⓐ The Supreme Court makes laws.

   Ⓑ The Supreme Court decides what a law means.

   Ⓒ The Supreme Court leads the government.

   Ⓓ The Supreme Court elects Congress.

2. How is the Supreme Court like an umpire in a game?

_____

_____

_____

Our Nation's Capital

1. Where is our nation's capital?

    Ⓐ in the Senate

    Ⓑ in the White House

    Ⓒ in Washington, D.C.

    Ⓓ in the Supreme Court building

2. Why might it be helpful for all three branches of government to work in the same place?

_____

_____

_____

Connect Your Ideas

1. What jobs do people have in each branch of government?

_____

_____

_____

2. Why do you think the government has three different branches?

_____

_____

_____

Reading Log • Level C • Book 1

	I Read This	New Words I Learned	New Facts I Learned	What Else I Want to Learn About This Subject
Dinosaurs				
Dinosaur Names				
Finding Out About Dinosaurs				
Meat-Eating Dinosaurs				
Plant-Eating Dinosaurs				
A Very Small Dinosaur				
Animal Giants				
Ocean Giants: Blue Whales				
Land Giants: Elephants				
Bird Giants: Ostriches				
Tall Giants: Giraffes				
Long Giants: Saltwater Crocodiles				
Plants				
The Parts of Plants				
How Plants Breathe				
Why Are Flowers Beautiful?				
Dangerous Plants				
Growing Your Own Plants				

	I Read This	New Words I Learned	New Facts I Learned	What Else I Want to Learn About This Subject
American Heroes				
George Washington				
Martin Luther King, Jr.				
Clara Barton				
César Chávez				
Wilma Rudolph				
Celebrations				
What Is a Celebration?				
Thanksgiving				
A Birthday Party for the United States				
Thinking About the Past				
Celebrating New Year's Day				
Our National Government				
Who's in Charge of Our Country?				
Leading the Way				
Making the Laws				
Helping People Understand the Laws				
Our Nation's Capital				

Self-Check Graph

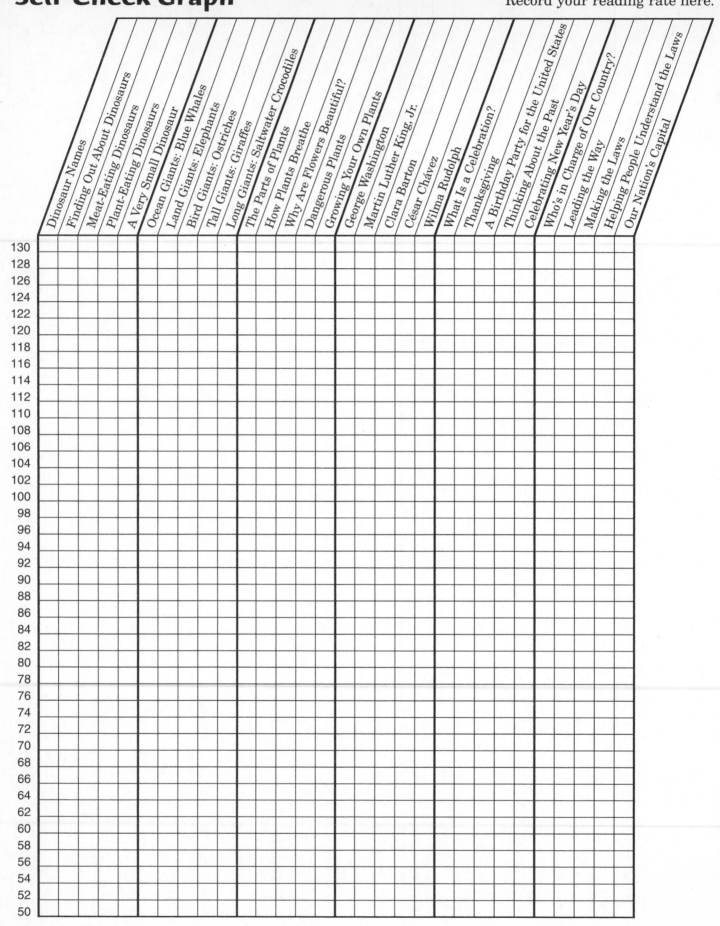